Famous Paintings

With 184 Plates, including 54 in Full Color

A Chanticleer Press Edition

Famous Paintings

An Introduction to Art

by Alice Elizabeth Chase

Yale University Art Gallery

PLATT & MUNK, *Publishers*

NEW YORK

Contents

The Magic World of Pictures

"Paintings must be looked at and looked at... They must be understood through the eyes," wrote an American painter. But it is not always easy to get to original paintings. They hang in public museums that may be many miles away, or in private collections that may seldom or never be open to visitors. A century ago the only way one could study a great painting was to travel to the place where it was shown—or buy one of the few (and often poor) copies that some other artist had painted or engraved.

Today, with modern photography and color reproduction, we can make prints like those shown in this book. Now anyone anywhere can own reproductions of works of art even though he may never be able to see the originals. Reproductions do not take the place of originals—the painting an artist worked on is unique—but they can make you familiar with a great number of paintings. Then, when you do see the originals in a museum, they will seem like old friends and you will be able to appreciate them fully.

Pictures are meant to be looked at, but we have two ways of looking—with our eyes and with our minds. Our eyes see only the surface—the lines, colors, and shapes. These may stir our feelings; for instance, sharp, angular lines and bright reds and yellows will excite us, while smooth curves, blues, and greens make us feel calm and rested. But when our minds help our eyes, we begin to understand as well as see. I would like to point out to you some of the things you can see with your mind.

Published in 1962 by The Platt & Munk Co., Inc., New York 10, N.Y. An earlier edition of this book was published in 1951. Prepared and produced in collaboration with Chanticleer Press Inc., New York. All rights reserved. Except for brief quotations in reviews, no part of this book may be reproduced without permission in writing from the publishers. This book is published simultaneously in the United States and Great Britain. Its entire contents are protected by copyright in all countries adhering to the Berne Convention. Text and plates printed by Rotogravure, Holland. Library of Congress Catalog Card Number: 62–9589

First of all there is the subject. The picture may show familiar scenes, objects, or people that you enjoy recognizing. Or it may tell a story, and you will want to find out what the story is. The way it is painted may have something to do with the times in which the artist lived, and it will be more interesting to you if you know something about those times. Or it may be the artist himself who is reflected in his work and you want to know something about him. Why did he paint this subject this way? What was he thinking about?

So as we look with our minds we find that a work of art is not only an arrangement of colors, lines, and shapes to give pleasure to our eyes but also a historical document like the Declaration of Independence, or the letters of Napoleon, which can tell us about a subject, a period, a country, or an artist—if we will take the trouble to read and learn.

Here in this book are almost two hundred pictures, some of them produced five thousand years ago, some within the last few years. In this edition twelve new pictures have been added, including four color plates of works by artists of our time—Picasso, Klee, Mondrian, and Stella. These artists paint the world of today, yet their subjects link with the art of the past. What theme is older than the one Picasso used—a mother and her child? How many artists through the centuries have enjoyed, as Stella did, the lure of roads and bridges? Fairy tale creatures are not more fantastic than Klee's bridges-that-walk. And even though Mondrian's painting may look totally new, rhythm in line and color is one of the basic principles of the art of all ages. So, different as they may be, these paintings too belong in the circle of famous paintings.

Works of art have personalities like human beings. Some of the pictures in this book will appeal to one person, some to another. You will like some of them better each time you look at them; others may cease to interest you. But if you take time, and look, and look again, you will find here a first step into a wonderful and magical world that can enrich your whole life.

New Haven, 1962   Alice Elizabeth Chase

"Let's Pretend"

Children love to dress up and play "pretend." Most often, perhaps, they pretend to be grown-ups, or kings, or princesses. Sir Joshua Reynolds liked the idea of painting little Master Crewe as Henry the Eighth. Everybody in England knew the picture of Henry that Hans Holbein had painted two hundred and fifty years before, and that you see on this page. It shows big, fat, obstinate, cruel Henry in the short full jacket, tights and stubtoed shoes of his time, standing with his feet wide apart and hands on hips. Master Crewe put on similar clothes and tried to take the same pose, but he is so little and merry that he almost laughs while Sir Joshua paints him. And we enjoy the joke too.

Many artists have painted children in dress-up clothes. A butcher's boy put on the silks of a century and a half earlier to become Gainsborough's *Blue Boy*. And Bellows' *Jean*, dressed in clothes of the 1890's, looks at you solemnly, as though to say, "You mustn't laugh, for I am not *little Jean* any more, but *Lady Jean!*"

Color Plate: Master Crewe as Henry VIII
   by Sir Joshua Reynolds (London,
   Collection of Lord O'Neill)

1 Lady Jean *by George Bellows*
2 The Blue Boy *by Thomas Gainsborough*
3 Henry VIII *after Hans Holbein*

First Steps

A child's first step is a milestone in his life. Up to then the baby has been completely dependent on his mother. With his first step he starts into the world and the tie to his mother begins to loosen. So, although she is happy and proud of his growth, there can be, for her, a touch of sadness in the moment.

This is the idea which Picasso presented in his painting. A number of vertical, horizontal and diagonal lines come together in the middle of the child's body, centering our attention on him. The mother stands solidly behind him, her figure broad and protecting—but she is only the background for the child. Her face spreads as though melting over him in complete absorption and concern. He, on the other hand, has no thought for her, but strikes out eagerly—eyes wide, nostrils expanded, mouth twisted with the effort. For him the first step is the beginning of freedom and great adventure; for her it is a warning that she will lose her child as he grows up.

Rembrandt, with a few swift strokes of the pen, makes us conscious of much the same things—the tender concern of the mother, the sturdy intentness of the child. To Millet the event was simply a homely scene; he was not concerned with deeper meanings.

Color Plate: First Steps *by Picasso* (New Haven, Yale University Art Gallery)

1 Learning to Walk: drawing *by Rembrandt*
2 First Steps: pastel *by Jean-François Millet*

11

"Sugar and Spice"

Some artists, when they paint people, make them look solid and heavy. Others show air and light and sun shimmering around them. Some make them quiet, with every detail clear. Others blur the details to suggest movement. Some try to show what kind of people they are, even what they are thinking about. Others are more interested in painting the clothes than the people inside them.

Here are five different pictures of little girls. Renoir's is sparkling in the fresh bright air of a sunny morning. She pauses for a moment. Nothing about her is done precisely. Her face, her hands, her dress are roughly painted, yet she looks alive. Crivelli's child is all intent curiosity. Precise lines emphasize how hard she is looking. We find ourselves wondering what she is looking at. For Frans Hals the clothes seem as important as the child, who is almost lost in the rich brocades. Cranach's *Princess* is just as elaborately dressed, but it is her shy little face that draws our interest. With little Miss Vigée-Lebrun it is what she is doing that catches our attention. She has tipped the mirror so that she can see us reflected in it, but all *we* can see is her own intent face. If you wonder whether a mirror really works like that, try it and see.

Color Plate: Child with Watering Can *by Pierre-Auguste Renoir* (Washington, National Gallery of Art)

1 Nurse and Child *by Frans Hals*
2 Princess of Saxony *by Lucas Cranach*
3 The Artist's Daughter *by Elisabeth Vigée-Lebrun*
4 Little Girl (detail from Annunciation) *by Carlo Crivelli*

Color Plate: The Dancing Couple *by*
Jan Steen (Washington, National Gallery
of Art)

1 Thread-the-Needle (La Kermesse)
by Peter Paul Rubens
2 Wedding Dance *by Pieter Bruegel*

14

1

Eating, Drinking and Dancing

In the Middle Ages only the Church and the nobility were wealthy enough to commission works of art. But gradually, with the growth of towns and the rise of a prosperous middle class, others were able to afford art works, and painters did fewer religious and aristocratic subjects and more scenes from everyday life. Paintings were also made smaller in size to fit the walls of private homes.

In the seventeenth century, after almost a hundred years of fighting, Holland won her independence from Spain, and the enthusiasm and energy of her people raised her to world leadership. in trade, industry, and art. It was the century of the Dutch East India Company, of the founding of New Amsterdam (now New York), of Rembrandt and Frans Hals, and of a host of other artists called "Little Masters" because their works were small. Their domestic scenes, still lifes, and landscapes were popular both at home and abroad, Vermeer, de Hooch and Brouwer (see pages 59, 47, 85) belonged to this group.

Jan Steen too was one of them. His favorite theme was people gathered in hall or courtyard for a good time. Being manager of an inn he had many opportunities to observe such occasions, and *The Dancing Couple* is typical of his paintings. Young and old are eating, drinking, or dancing, all in the best of humors. A mother, perhaps Jan Steen's own wife, plays with her baby who holds a wooden toy such as we sometimes still see today. The scene looks noisy but full of hearty fun.

Among the first to paint peasants at play was Pieter Bruegel, whose *Wedding Dance* is the ancestor of such works as this by Steen and of *La Kermesse* by Rubens.

15

Children and Pets

Like other artists of the eighteenth century Goya painted only the well-dressed children of the upper classes, but he knew and loved children (he had twenty of his own) and no artist has caught more convincingly the wistfulness of childhood. Don Manuel stands absorbed with steady, thoughtful eyes. He has forgotten for the moment the caged birds, the tethered magpie and the three cats. There is nothing soft or sentimental about Goya's painting. The colors are vigorous and the body is solid and carefully rendered. The stare of the cats contrasts with the look of the child, his innocent, theirs viciously purposeful, as they watch for an opportunity to jump on the bird.

Hogarth, fifty years before Goya, brought a caged bird and a marvelously expressive cat into his painting of the Graham children. In contrast to Don Manuel the Graham children are active. The boy, his face bright with pleasure, cranks his music box while his sister gaily spreads her skirts to dance. The cat on the back of the chair is as tense as a coiled spring.

The pet fawn in the portrait of the little De Peyster boy of old New York, by an unknown artist, suggests the artist's desire to emphasize the grace and shyness of the child. Stiff as he may seem in his extraordinary clothes, the boy has a gentle charm.

Color Plate: Don Manuel Osorio *by Francisco Goya* (New York, Metropolitan Museum of Art)

1 Boy with a Deer *by an unknown American artist*
2 The Graham Children *by William Hogarth*

Music in Paint

Music has magic in it. If we are tired and cross it can rest us and charm us into good humor. When we dawdle, music may stir us to faster and harder work. Sometimes as we listen, pictures unfold before our mind's eye.

Chagall's *Snowing* translates one of these mind pictures into paint. We are not at all sure what it means, but it is unexpected and gay. A purple-clad clown with a green hand and leg is fiddling under a night sky amid the snowflakes in the street of a Russian village. His music does not seem to have aroused anyone in the houses, but it has brought forth a strange part-human creature with blue donkey's head and white fairy wings. What he represents we can only guess, but even if we are not sure we can still enjoy the picture as a phantasy.

Other artists have pictured the magic of music in other ways. Almost a thousand years ago an unknown painter showed David playing his harp to his flocks. Behind him sits a woman representing Melody, and in the corners are the spirits of mountain and rock, all three conjured up by the beauty of his music. The Greeks and Romans liked to tell of Orpheus who tamed wild beasts with his playing and made even stones listen. And the modern Nura paints a little girl with cherub wings and an angelic expression who accompanies three gay little birds that twitter above her.

Color Plate: Snowing
  by Marc Chagall (St. Louis, City Art Museum)

1 Orpheus Charming Animals: Roman catacomb painting, 3rd century
  (Illustrated in Bosio, *Roma Sotterranea*, 1632)
2 Harmony *by Nura*
3 David Playing the Harp: from the Paris Psalter, 10th century

19

Soldier Saints

The warrior saints who were ready to shield the innocent and fight the enemies of God were much beloved by the faithful. First in popularity came St. George (see page 67) who had saved the princess from the dragon. Another popular soldier saint was St. Maurice, sometimes pictured as a Moor. Maurice was an officer in the Roman army. Though Christian, he and his legion obeyed their pagan Roman master until they were ordered to sacrifice to heathen idols and join in the slaughter of Christians. This they refused to do, and more than six thousand of them, says the legend, suffered martyrdom. St. Eustace, another Roman soldier, was devoted to hunting until, one day, he saw a stag bearing the Crucifix between its horns. Eustace immediately turned from his worldly ways and was converted.

Almost as beloved as St. George was St. Martin of Tours, who was noted for acts of kindness and generosity. During one exceptionally cold winter many people suffered from want. St. Martin had given away his last coin when he met a beggar, half-naked and shivering. Having nothing left to give except his own clothing, the Saint drew his sword and divided his cloak with the beggar. That night as he sat at dinner a strange king entered the hall wearing the half cloak. It was Christ Himself, come to thank him.

Against a sky filled with threatening clouds, El Greco sets the slender, aristocratic saint and the starving beggar. The elongation of the figures, including the horse, seems to lift them out of the everyday world into a realm of lofty thoughts and noble deeds.

Color Plate: St. Martin and the Beggar
by El Greco (Washington,
National Gallery of Art)

1 St. Maurice (right wing of Adoration of Magi) *by Hans Baldung*
2 St. George and the Dragon (detail) *by Vittore Carpaccio*
3 The Vision of St. Eustace *by Pisanello*

21

Horses, Horses, Horses

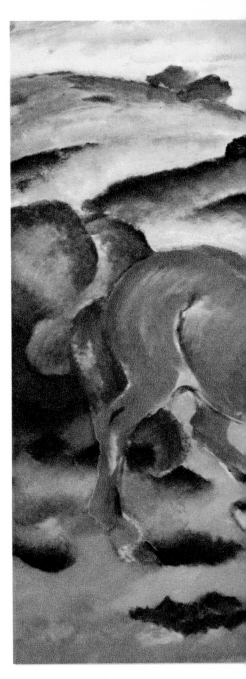

"I never saw a purple cow, I never hope to see one," wrote a famous humorist, and I might add that I also never expect to see red horses in real life. But if I do, I hope they will be cavorting around a field with blue rocks and orange bushes under a yellow sky just like these.

Franz Marc purposely used such unusual colors in order to tell us more about horses than just what they look like. The red indicates something of their vigor, their alertness and intelligence. From the smooth, flowing curves of their necks and backs and hind quarters we sense the grace of their movements.

Many have delighted in representing horses. Some ancient Assyrian more than six hundred years before Christ watched a horse hunt and recorded in stone relief on the palace wall the anxious way a mare turned to see if her colt was escaping the pursuing dog. Using line alone, a Japanese artist conveys the springy power of horses galloping over a field. To the Persian who drew the *Four Horses* the curves of the animals' necks and backs gave the idea for this puzzle picture in which you can see two horses facing each other and two back to back, though there are only two heads and eight legs.

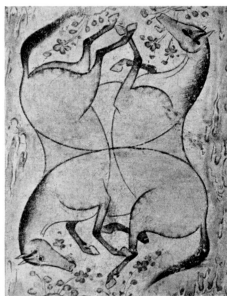

Color Plate: Red Horses
by Franz Marc (Essen,
Folkwang-Museum)

1 Four Horses: Persian drawing,
  17th century
2 Wild Horses: Assyrian relief
  (detail), 7th century B.C.
3 Horses *by Toba Sojo*

The Victorious Wrestler

Hercules, the strong man of Greek and Roman mythology, had many adventures in which his great strength assured him victory. As a baby, he strangled two serpents as shown in the painting from Pompeii. When grown up, he undertook twelve "labors," each more difficult than the last. The first was killing a lion. From its skin he made himself a cloak, which, along with his great club, helps us recognize him in paintings and sculptures. The second labor was destroying the hydra, a fearful, nine-headed dragon.

On a journey into a far land to secure some golden apples, Hercules met Antaeus, an evil giant who slew travelers. Antaeus was a son of Earth and as long as his feet were planted on her, he could not be overcome. With superhuman strength Hercules lifted him off the ground and squeezed the life out of him.

Hercules killing Antaeus was a popular subject in the Renaissance. It gave artists a fine opportunity to study muscles and show the human body in action. It was also a symbol of the triumph of good over evil. Tintoretto suggests this symbolism by making the two figures large against the sky and by curving the ground under Hercules' feet. In conquering Antaeus, Hercules conquers the earth. He is man triumphant.

1

2

Color Plate: Hercules and Antaeus *by Tintoretto* (Hartford, Wadsworth Athenaeum)

1 Infant Hercules Strangling Serpents (detail): Roman painting, 1st century

2 Hercules and the Hydra *by Antonio del Pollaiuolo*

25

Things Alive

Viaducts (first used by the ancient Romans) are becoming more and more familiar in our own landscape. They support the highways that carry through-traffic above our city streets. They bridge rivers and stretch over deep valleys. The arches that hold them up are sometimes high and narrow and at other times squat. Their solidity contrasts with the flashing movement of the cars above. So it is indeed a revolution when the viaducts themselves begin to move! Under Klee's brush the concrete columns become legs that walk. They leave their fixed rows and stride about, some tall and thin, some short and stocky, variously colored as though wearing tights. Although they have neither heads nor hearts, they have come alive. Klee has whimsically transformed them into new and startling shapes.

Other artists see in the structures and machines of our mechanical age something that contradicts the human qualities of love and sympathy. Fernand Léger constructed figures out of shapes and colors that look like girders and pipes—cold, hard, and soulless. Max Ernst covered a wooden ground with wet plaster, roughened it to the texture of a wall, then drew on it in gray and black an arrangement of blocks which become a human being. Without arms or neck, with a single rivet-like eye, the artist has here created a stiff, soulless, and powerful automaton.

Color Plate: Revolution of the Viaduct
  by Paul Klee (Hamburg, Kunsthalle)

1 Anthropomorphic Figure *by Max Ernst*
  (New Haven, Yale University Art
  Gallery)

2 Three Women or Le Grand Déjeuner
  by Fernand Léger (New York, Museum
  of Modern Art)

26

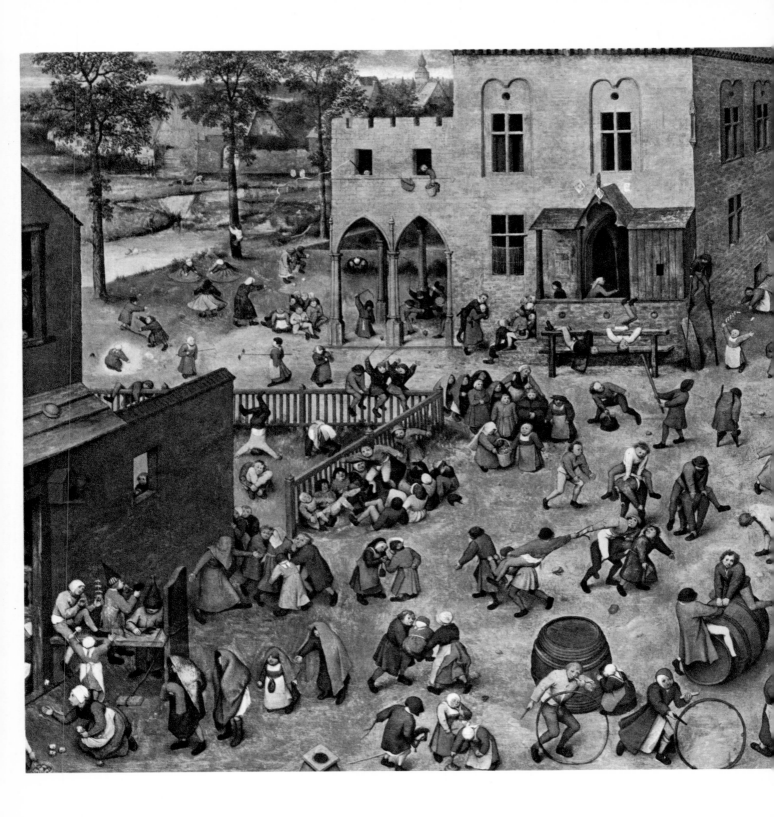

Color Plate: Children's Games *by Pieter Bruegel* (Vienna, Kunsthistorisches Muse[...]

1 Girls Playing Jackstones: Roman paintin[...] on marble, 1st century
2 Boy with a Kite (detail) *by John Zoffany*
3 The Spielers *by George Luks*

Playing Games

Children's games change little through the ages. In Bruegel's sixteenth-century painting we recognize games that were played in ancient Rome (see Roman painting above) and that are still popular today. In the bottom left corner girls are tossing "jacks" (only they use knucklebones instead). A little farther along a boy rides his hobbyhorse. To his right two boys are rolling hoops. Near the center is a tug of war and beyond that are boys playing leapfrog. Around the fence come little girls dressed up to play "wedding." Boys walk on stilts; girls play blindman's buff; boys and girls together spin tops, roll marbles, and play tag. In the distance children are swimming, some using water-wings. At least seventy different games are going on. The only grown person is the woman at the side window of the big house throwing water on two boys who are fighting.

How does Bruegel avoid confusion in such a busy scene? By carefully spacing the groups and by leaving out shadows and confusing details he makes the games as clear as things in a showcase. But he was so busy getting them all in that he forgot to make them look like fun. George Luks' little girls are bubbling over with happiness. We are not sure just what they are doing, but we know they are having a wonderful time. Zoffany's *Boy with a Kite* looks happy, too, but he is so dressed up we wonder whether he is really playing or just posing for his picture.

2

3

1

2

Group Pictures

In the days before cameras, when people wanted a picture of their club or team, it had to be painted by an artist. He would sketch an arrangement for the group and paint the figures from hired models. Then each person would pose for the painting of his own head and pay his share of the cost. Some artists, like Ter Borch, in *The Congress of Münster,* produced dull rows of people like so many ninepins. Hals, with more originality, arranged club members around a table as though they had just finished dinner.

Captain Banning Cocq got the finest artist in Amsterdam, Rembrandt van Rijn, to paint the company of war veterans which he commanded. Rembrandt pictured the men as though just coming out of a meeting. A streak of light falling between two buildings strikes some of them. A little girl in the middle of the street seems to have just happened by on the way home from market with a chicken for dinner.

Rembrandt worked on the painting for many months. When the company came to inspect it they found much to criticize. The picture was too big. The little girl did not belong there. Some of the faces were half hidden. The painting was so dark that it looked like a night picture—hence the nickname *The Night Watch*. They accepted it reluctantly.

Now, three centuries later, we remember Captain Cocq and his men only because they appear in this painting. They were right—it is not a good picture of the members of a company. But it is a magnificent study of light and shadow, of deep space and many figures subtly related through variations in color.

Color Plate: The Sortie of Captain Banning Cocq's Company, called The Night Watch, *by Rembrandt* (Amsterdam, Rijksmuseum)

1 Officers of St. George's Company *by Frans Hals*
2 The Congress of Münster *by Gerard Ter Borch*

31

1

2

Color Plate: The Gulf Stream
by Winslow Homer (New York,
Metropolitan Museum of Art)

1 Christ on the Sea of Galilee
by Eugène Delacroix

2 A Miracle of St. Nicholas of
Tolentino *by Giovanni di Paolo*

Storm at Sea

A lone survivor, groggy from storm and weak with hunger, lies on the deck of his battered sloop. Mast, rudder, hatch, have washed away, and circling sharks are waiting for him to slip helpless off the sloping deck. In the distance looms a "twister."

It is easy to think only of the story, to wonder if that shadowy ship on the horizon will sight the derelict in time; but what absorbed Winslow Homer was the quality of sky and water, the vivid wetness of boat and fish, the foam of rolling whitecaps.

Giovanni di Paolo tells his story without concern for realism. "The sea was rough," he seems to say, "the masts broke, the sails blew away. We prayed to St. Nicholas and he stilled the storm." In spite of splintered masts and flying sails, the ship seems steady and safe. The waves through which the mermaid swims look like rocky peaks.

Delacroix's *Christ on the Sea of Galilee* approaches the subject of storm at sea from another point of view. The pictured waves are not enough to explain the gestures of cowering and fright. Delacroix is trying to tell us that the worst storm is the one within the faithless soul who does not believe that Jesus, asleep in the bow, can really save him. So Delacroix's scene is not copied from nature, like Homer's, or based on set conventions, like Giovanni di Paolo's, but is an expression of human feeling.

"Sit Like an Apple"

Placing massive figures in relationship to each other in space is what interested Cézanne in painting this picture. The four peasants around the card table are as solid and real as though they were rocks. Every shape, color, and line in the picture has a purpose. Notice the rectangles of the table, its legs and drawer, the smooth broad curves of the men's shoulders and backs, the semicircles of their hats. You can feel the space in the room—exactly how deep the table is, just where the man with the red scarf is standing between the players and the wall.

Cézanne was acquainted with Monet, the Impressionist (see page 99). When Monet's painting of flowers is reproduced without color we feel that the most important thing has been left out. Cézanne wanted to keep the bright color of Impressionism but make of it "something solid like the paintings in the museums." He worked very slowly. People often posed for him a hundred times, many hours each time, and if they moved he would shout savagely, "Sit like an apple!" He liked to paint apples because they could not move, and did not rot quickly, and he could take as much time as he needed.

Other French artists have also been interested in the shapes of things, among them Chardin (see page 43) whom Cézanne admired and from whose painting he learned much.

1

2

Color Plate: The Card Players *by Paul Cézanne* (New York, Metropolitan Museum of Art, Stephen C. Clark Bequest)

1 Chrysanthemums *by Claude Monet*
2 Apples and Pears *by Paul Cézanne*

The Saint who Preached to the Birds

Of all Italian painters the Venetians, particularly, loved the outdoors. Rocks, grass, trees, water, houses, all interested them, but especially light and air. They make us feel it around us, bright and warm. It becomes a glowing setting for flowers, animals, birds, and people. In this picture the vine growing over the trellis outside the cave, the flowers in the crannies of the cliff, the donkey standing contented on the grass, the town, the hillside, and even the clouds are bathed in it.

St. Francis loved all nature—he even preached to birds and fishes—but here his attention is absorbed by something else. You know his story: how he gave all he had to the poor and spent his life in service to man and beast; how finally Christ appeared to him in a vision and impressed the marks of the nails on the Saint's hands and feet in recognition of his goodness. This is the moment that Bellini shows: St. Francis standing, his whole being concentrated on the vision which we cannot see. Dürer includes it, even drawing lines from Christ's hands and feet to the Saint's to indicate the miracle.

St. Francis may always be recognized in art (see all the pictures on these two pages) by his gray-brown garment, his rope belt, his bare or sandaled feet, and the scars—called the stigmata—in his hands and feet.

Color Plate: St. Francis in Ecstasy *by Giovanni Bellini* (New York, Frick Collection)

1 St. Francis Preaching to the Birds *by Giotto*
2 St. Francis Receives the Stigmata: drawing *by Albrecht Dürer*
3 St. Francis (detail from altarpiece) *by Pietro Perugino*

People Working

Seeing people working in the fields or carrying loads on their backs, have you noticed the steady, measured way they move, the sturdy solidity of their bodies?

Rivera is a Mexican painter, part Spanish, part Indian, and he often watched peasants going about their work. He studied in Mexico, in Spain, and in France, but he never felt at home painting forms that dissolved in colored light, as did the Impressionists, or that were changed into geometric shapes, as did the Cubists. He was used to the clear air and bright sun of Mexico, where objects look sharp-edged and solid. Finally he decided to return to his native land and paint the life he knew best. On the way home he traveled through Italy where the fourteenth-century frescoes of Giotto impressed him strongly. Giotto knew no more about anatomy than the Egyptian sculptor who had carved the *Woman Grinding* some 4000 years earlier, but he understood how to give figures substance. His painting of the Italian nobleman, Enrico Scrovegno, presenting a chapel to three angels gives typical examples of his figures— simple, solid and convincing. Rivera learned from his own observation of people at work, from paintings such as Giotto's or Millet's, and from ancient sculpture, that bodies can be simplified to large cylinders, arms and legs to smaller cylinders, heads to round knobs, and that by painting them this way and not bothering with details one can convey something of the character of labor and laborer. Like Giotto and Michelangelo, Rivera worked in fresco, that is, directly on wet plaster walls. Perhaps no one has rendered better than he the sturdy simplicity of the Mexican people.

Color Plate: The Flower Vendor *by Diego Rivera* (San Francisco, Museum of Art)

1 Woman Grinding: Egyptian sculpture, about 2700 B.C.
2 The Gleaners *by Jean-François Millet*
3 Scrovegno Presents the Arena Chapel (detail from Last Judgment) *by Giotto*

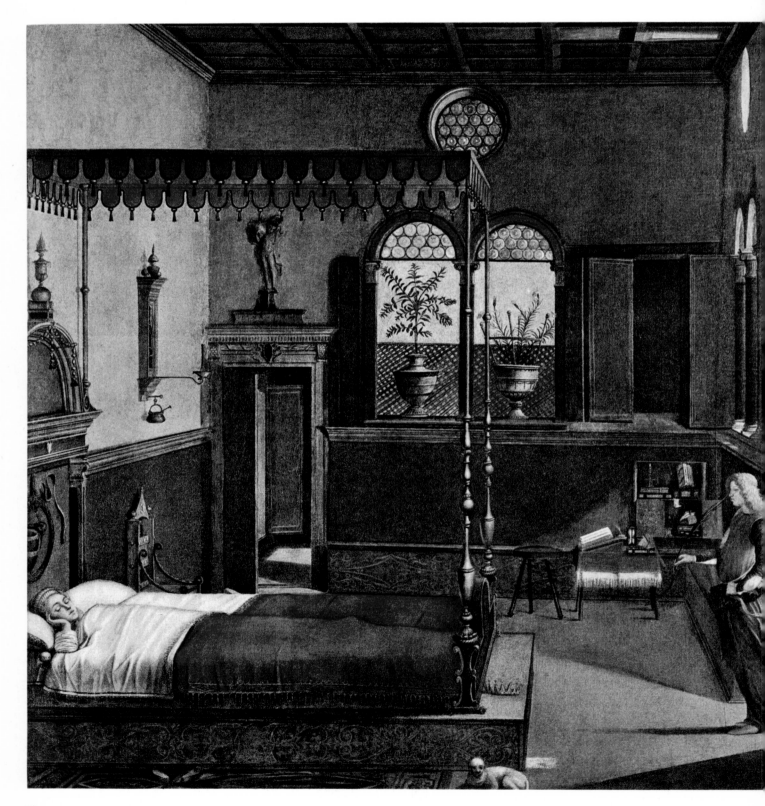

Saints at Home

Little St. Ursula has finally reached Rome, the goal of her pilgrimage. Now, her duty done, she can dream of returning to her father's kingdom and marrying the prince to whom she is engaged. But no! As she sleeps, an angel comes to her bearing the palm of martyrdom. We are dismayed at the thought. But as we look at her calm face we remember that, to a medieval pilgrim, martyrdom was the highest possible honor.

The story is gently told. The angel does not even disturb the dog watching by his mistress' bed. Quietness and peace are suggested by the vertical and horizontal lines of the room, and by its perfect order. St. Ursula's little blue slippers lie under the bed. Plants grow at an open window, and the morning sun streams in.

People of the Middle Ages pictured the saints in surroundings like their own. St. Ursula's bedroom belongs in an Italian palace. Dürer's St. Jerome works in a study such as might have been used by a German scholar of Dürer's own time, and Robert Campin shows a Flemish St. Joseph in his workshop making mousetraps!

Color Plate: St. Ursula's Dream *by Vittore Carpaccio* (Venice, Academy)

St. Joseph at Work: right wing of altarpiece *by Robert Campin, the Master of Flémalle*
St. Jerome in his Study: engraving *by Albrecht Dürer*

Little Men and Women

Color Plate: Boy with a Top *by J.B.S.Chardin* (Paris, Louvre)

1 Daniel Ver Planck with a Flying Squirrel *by John Singleton Copley*
2 Princess Margareta Theresa *by Velásquez*
3 Filippo Cattaneo *by Sir Anthony Van Dyck*

Dressed in the fashions of their parents, these children of seventeenth—or eighteenth—century merchants, noblemen or kings look like miniature men and women. It is plain that they were kept by costume as well as custom from enjoying the kind of carefree games children enjoy today. Chardin liked to show them at play, but a sedate play that could be carried on at a table without muss or dirt. Chardin understood children and enjoyed their concentration on the activity of the moment. The elegant little boy with curled and powdered hair and tightly buttoned waistcoat is absorbed in his spinning top. Like Cézanne a century and half later (see page 34), Chardin was interested in the relations of forms: in the rectangular table with its partly open drawer, in the books apparently thrown down casually yet actually placed with great care, in the inkwell repeating and varying the shape of the top, and in the graceful, solid figure of the child.

Van Dyck's seven-year-old is a miniature man in pose and expression as well as in costume; and Velásquez' little Princess Margareta, who later married the Emperor of Austria, looks already a queen. Daniel Ver Planck, child of an aristocratic family of colonial America, is precisely painted in tight-fitting clothes, sitting in the conventional landscape which the artist, Copley, had learned from English engravings.

Tu-re-lu-re-lu, pat-a-pat-a-pan

"When you hear the fife and drum, dance and make the village hum." So runs an old French Christmas carol. Pipe and drum of one sort or another have contributed to people's festivities down through the centuries. The ancient Greeks played the double pipes for religious dances, the drumbeats being provided by castanets in the hands of the dancers. Medieval shepherds whiled away their time in the fields with recorders and bagpipes, and for drums they used hollowed logs covered with hide. We see them with their instruments, kneeling in adoration of the infant Jesus. Brought into town, pipe and drum added to the merriment of an evening in the tavern or cheered soldiers on their weary marches. Fife and drum corps still have a part in military parades.

So when Manet dressed his little model in an oversize uniform and gave him a fife to play, he was using a familiar theme. His interest, however, was less in the subject than in the pattern of the red trousers, blue coat, and gold-trimmed hat against the gray background. He liked the flat areas of color that earlier artists got simply by omitting shadows. Like Degas (see page 92) he studied Japanese prints. But Manet was a realist who believed he must see what he painted. He turned on all the gas lights in his studio and painted the boy in the bright glare, the red of his clothes heightened by the color of the gas flame, his roundness flattened as an actor is by the footlights of a stage.

Color Plate: The Fifer *by Edouard Manet* (Paris, Louvre)

1 Musician Playing Double Pipes: Greek vase (detail), 6th century B.C.

2 Shepherds with Bagpipe (detail from Adoration of Shepherds) *by Jean Fouquet*

3 Piper and Drummer (detail from altarpiece) *by Albrecht Dürer*

"Squared Away"

The people who lived in these houses were solid, middle-class merchants. The artists tell us this by emphasizing squares and rectangles, repeated as steadily as the beat in a march. You know how we use the word "square" to mean *good* and *honest*—as when we speak of a "square deal" or eating a "square meal." To keep us from getting tired of these squares Pieter de Hooch and Janssens tip some sideways, in the door, the chairs, and the pictures and mirror on the wall. The tiles on the floor, turned diagonally, become diamond-shaped. The rooms themselves are blocks opening from one to the other, one dark, the next well lit, the next dark, and so on.

Only live things are outlined in curves: the people and the dog. Notice the curves of the little boy and his mother, of the women at work in Vermeer's *Dutch Street*. Notice, especially, the wonderful balance of straight lines and curves in Rembrandt's *Girl at a Half Door*. She stands squarely in the middle of the rectangular opening, but her head, shoulders, arms and skirt are a series of curves.

These paintings show the houses and people that the Pilgrims knew when they stopped in Holland on their way to the New World. From such homes came the emigrants who founded old New Amsterdam, where you can imagine steep-roofed houses like these built close to the streets, and half-open Dutch doors giving glimpses of clean tiled floors and sturdy furniture.

Color Plate: Inside of a House *by Pieter de Hooch* (London, Wallace Collection)

1 Dutch Street *by Jan Vermeer*
2 Girl at a Half Door *by Rembrandt*
3 Dutch Interior *by Pieter Janssens*

46

Patterns in Color

Matisse saw this woman in a green skirt beside a vase of flowers on a blue couch with orange pillows as a pattern in flat colors. To give a refreshing sense of having painted casually and quickly he drew broad, heavy outlines or scratched in ornamental details. Features are sketched roughly. He purposely avoided suggesting depth—he wanted his picture to be as flat as wallpaper or the design on a curtain. The result is that there are no shadows, the couch is not in perspective, the table top seems tipped up. Nothing matters but the areas of color and their relation to each other. Delicate, transparent shades are balanced against heavy tones. Notice the slightly different shades of blue, the glowing oranges and lemon placed so casually on the table yet so important to the whole. Try covering up the lemon and notice how much life the picture loses. "What is Matisse trying to say?" you ask. Simply that color can do through the eye what music does through the ear—refresh the human spirit.

An unknown French tapestry-maker of the early sixteenth century placed his violinist against a background sprinkled with flowers. He was as interested in formal elegance and grace as in color and pattern. By contrast, the Impressionist Degas (see also page 92) wanted his painting to look like the record of what he saw with a quick glance—flowers, fresh from the garden, and the woman waiting beside them absorbed in her thoughts.

Color Plate: Anemones and
    Woman: Harmony in
    Blue *by Henri Matisse*
    (Private Collection)

1 A Concert (detail):
    French tapestry, about
    1500
2 Woman with Chrysan-
    themums *by Edgar Degas*

The Smile

1

2

Leonardo, born in the little town of Vinci near Florence, was one of the greatest artists that ever lived. He was also a great scientist. Everything interested him—engineering projects, war machines, mathematics, geology, medicine. He was fascinated by the way creatures move and he tried to learn exactly how muscles work.

One of his most famous paintings is the portrait of Madonna Lisa del Giocondo, called *Mona Lisa* for short. Legend has it that music, played while she posed, charmed the curious smile to her lips. Leonardo's scientific mind seems to have delighted in rendering the muscles under the skin and in modeling the surface with the utmost delicacy. Is the smile in the mouth or in the eyes? Can we read it in the cheeks? Mona Lisa's hands were executed with as much care as her face, and have been called the most beautiful hands in painting.

What of other smiles in art? Early Greek sculptors curved the lips in a set smile to indicate that their subjects were alive. No muscles seem to work under the stone surface. *The Laughing Cavalier's* smile is mostly in the eyes, the turned-up moustache, and the great upward sweep of the hat. In Desiderio's *Laughing Boy* the whole face laughs: mouth, cheeks, eyes, even forehead— and it is such a catching laugh that we laugh too.

Color Plate: Mona Lisa *by Leonardo da Vinci* (Paris, Louvre)

1 Laughing Boy: sculpture *by Desiderio da Settignano*
2 Head of Megakles: Greek funeral monument (detail), 6th century B.C.
3 The Laughing Cavalier (detail) *by Frans Hals*

Shrimp Girl

Hogarth usually painted slowly and carefully, but one day he dashed off a sketch of a girl he had seen that morning in the fish market—healthy, happy, with bright eyes and rosy cheeks. Someone had called to her and she had turned quickly, her basket of shrimps on her head. For this sketch Hogarth used big brushes and daubed the paint on roughly. It probably took him less than an hour. The paint is thick and the canvas shows through, but the girl looks so alive that you can almost hear the call that stopped her and made her turn to listen. She is as vivid as if she were painted yesterday.

Frans Hals did the same sort of thing a hundred years before Hogarth; and Velásquez, in Spain, loved to paint in a similar way. A century after Hogarth, Manet did it, too. We call all these paintings "impressionistic"—records of a moment, a passing expression, a glimpse. If they were done with fine, smooth brush strokes and finished in every detail they would be spoiled—the quickness would be gone. As it is, they seem almost alive.

Color Plate: The Shrimp Girl *by William Hogarth* (London, National Gallery)

1 The Fisher Girl *by Frans Hals*
2 Portrait of Line Campineau *by Edouard Manet*
3 Head of Spinola (detail from Surrender of Breda) *by Velásquez*

1 Boys Wrestling: relief from an Egyptian
  tomb, about 2500 B.C.
2 Hercules and Antaeus: sculpture *by Antonio
  del Pollaiuolo*
3 Wrestlers: Greek sculpture, about 200 B.C.

Color Plate: Stag at Sharkey's *by George
  Bellows* (Cleveland, Museum of Art)

1

In the Ring

Artists have always enjoyed watching human beings in action and trying to transfer that action to wall or canvas. Sports offer endless opportunity for such study and among the oldest of popular sports is wrestling or boxing. Some ancient Egyptian recorded a wrestling match in a series of pictures showing special holds. They are not scenes of action so much as descriptive diagrams, each labeled in Egyptian writing. The Greeks studied the human body in order to depict it both accurately and ideally, that is, they combined all the best qualities of individuals harmoniously to produce the perfect man. The shapes and movements in the *Wrestlers* are carefully balanced against each other. The Renaissance artist's interest in straining bodies is seen in Pollaiuolo's *Hercules and Antaeus,* in which the two figures look almost as if they had been skinned.

George Bellows, a twentieth-century American, used to like to drop in at Sharkey's Athletic Club on West 66th Street in New York City and watch the fights. They were pretty rough and therefore "stag," that is, for men only. Above all they were tense with excitement and it was this excitement of action that Bellows wanted to paint rather than the specific blows or muscle play. He concentrated on the spotlighted ring and the curves of the glistening bodies contrasted with the straight lines of the ropes. He did not copy any one pose but invented an arrangement which would give us the sense of seeing the whole fight in a single picture. The heads of the spectators rising out of the blackness around the ring make us aware that we are not the only watchers, but do not distract our attention from the three men under the lights.

Color Plate: The Fighting Téméraire
  by J.M.W. Turner (London,
  National Gallery)

1 The Embarkation of the Queen of
  Sheba *by Claude Lorrain*
2 Peace: Burial at Sea
  by J.M.W. Turner

"Going West"

The *Téméraire* was the second ship of the line of Lord Nelson's fleet. In the famous battle of Trafalgar where many an English ship was destroyed by the French, the *Téméraire* fought side by side with the flagship till victory was won. Then she came home and anchored proudly in the Thames. But she was old and badly damaged. New and faster ships were built and the famous old "fighting" *Téméraire* became a nuisance, occupying needed space. Word came down that she should be destroyed. So the old ship, symbol of past glory, was nudged out into the channel by a noisy, smoking little tug and taken to the wrecker.

This is the story that Turner wanted to tell. Moreover, he wanted to express the pathos of old age and uselessness. He painted the ship against the sunset. The red clouds recall the violent battles in which she has taken part; but it is a peaceful red now, and the waters are quiet. Her spars glow against the sky as if she were already a ghost ship.

Turner painted many sunset pictures. He liked the warm colors and the sense of peace and quiet that comes with the end of the day. From a French artist, Claude Lorrain, he had learned the effectiveness of a bright sky and setting sun and, in *Burial at Sea*, he again used them to express a wistful sadness.

Cooks and Kitchens

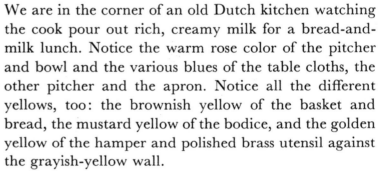

We are in the corner of an old Dutch kitchen watching the cook pour out rich, creamy milk for a bread-and-milk lunch. Notice the warm rose color of the pitcher and bowl and the various blues of the table cloths, the other pitcher and the apron. Notice all the different yellows, too: the brownish yellow of the basket and bread, the mustard yellow of the bodice, and the golden yellow of the hamper and polished brass utensil against the grayish-yellow wall.

It is fun to look at each object in this picture, to enjoy the color and the "feel" of it even though you can't really touch it. But the light is the most interesting of all. It comes through the window and flows over everything, making shadows and reflections. The whole back wall is softly illuminated and sets off the dark edge of the cook's shoulder and skirt so clearly that we know exactly where she is standing—halfway between us and the wall.

Many artists have painted foods and dishes. Chardin's nurse pauses beside a well-laid table. Pieter Aertsen shows a busy kitchen with open fireplace. Both he and Cornelis Cruys loved polished kettles, bright china, and wonderful foods, as good to look at as to taste.

Color Plate: The Cook *by Jan Vermeer* (Amsterdam, Rijksmuseum)

1 The Rich Feast *by Pieter Aertsen*
2 Breakfast Still Life *by Cornelis Cruys*
3 Food for the Convalescent *by J. B. S. Chardin*

Famous Actresses

An artist who wishes to paint an actress has to decide whether to paint her as she really is or to paint the person she pretends to be when she acts. Or he may try to make us see in one picture both herself and the parts she plays.

Mrs. Siddons was one of the greatest actresses of the late eighteenth and early nineteenth centuries. Gainsborough painted a handsome woman with beautiful skin, strong features and a nose so long that he is said finally to have thrown down his brushes exclaiming, "Madam, is there no end to your nose?" She wears the clothes fashionable in her day; a great hat, a rich silk dress with blue stripes, a pink shawl, and carries a fur muff. But why is she so impressive? Perhaps it is that she occupies so much of the canvas, or perhaps it is the arrangement of the cool grays and blues of her hair and dress against the reds of the background, or perhaps it is the steady look of her eyes. Somehow we realize that she is both a beautiful woman and a great one.

Sir Joshua Reynolds painted Mrs. Siddons, too, but as a sort of goddess—the Tragic Muse. She is all actress. When Sargent painted Ellen Terry in 1889 he chose to show her as Lady Macbeth, the part she was acting. In Eugene Speicher's *Katharine Cornell,* as in Gainsborough's *Mrs. Siddons* we see both the beautiful woman and the great actress.

1

Color Plate: Mrs. Siddons
  by Thomas Gainsborough
  (London, National Gallery)

1 Mrs. Siddons as the Tragic
  Muse *by Sir Joshua Reynolds*
2 Ellen Terry as Lady Macbeth
  by John Singer Sargent
3 Katharine Cornell as Candida
  by Eugene Speicher

2

3

Artists Look at Themselves

The cheapest and handiest subject for an artist to paint is *himself,* for all he needs is a mirror and his tools. He may choose to paint exactly what he sees or he may try to set down what he is thinking about or how he feels.

Van Gogh was an intense, emotional person with few friends, happy only when he was painting. He had periods of mental illness during the last two years of his life and in this picture his face shows signs of nervous strain. He loved color and laid it on in broad, bright strokes. Orange beard and greenish flesh, yellow hair and blue coat—these contrasting colors startle one, yet this placing of opposites side by side emphasizes both the brilliance of the colors and the conflict that we know went on within the man behind the piercing eyes.

Rembrandt was interested in light and shadow. He used them not only to give roundness to his figure but also to suggest moods. In his self-portrait we sense the discouragement and loneliness that he experienced as he grew older.

Other artists have been more cheerful. Chardin drew himself just as he looked, glasses, eyeshade, and all. Mme Vigée-Lebrun included her palette and brushes so that we seem to see her at work.

Color Plate: Portrait of the Artist *by Vincent Van Gogh* (Laren, Collection of V.W. Van Gogh)

1 Self-Portrait *by Elisabeth Vigée-Lebrun*
2 Self-Portrait *by J.B.S. Chardin*
3 Self-Portrait *by Rembrandt*

Small Princes

"Little one, become like your father, be heir to the virtue of him whose equal the world does not possess. Heaven and earth could hardly produce a son to surpass in glory such a father." This is a translation of part of the inscription under the picture of the child who was to become King Edward VI. Young Edward might have had trouble surpassing his father in fame, but not in virtue. Of his father, Henry VIII, a rhymester wrote:

"King Henry the Eighth to six wives was wedded,
One died, one survived, two divorced, two beheaded."

But Edward VI died at sixteen, so soon after he became king that he had little time to show what sort of ruler he could be. Holbein, the court painter, makes him look every inch a king's son. His rich brocaded silks, his erect pose, his serious face with its firm mouth and steady gaze mark him as different from an ordinary two-year-old. Only the gold rattle in his hand suggests that he was allowed any of the privileges of babyhood.

Henry II, who came to the throne of France the same year Edward became king of England, was a weak and bigoted ruler. As a baby, in Clouet's painting, he looks innocent enough. When the baby Van Dyck shows became James II of England, he was so hated that he was eventually deposed and exiled. Legend tells us that the Medici princeling, Don Garcia, son of Duke Cosimo I of Florence, murdered his own brother. It is hard to believe that of the jolly three-year-old we see here.

Color Plate: Edward VI as a Child *by Hans Holbein* (Washington, National Gallery of Art)

1 Don Garcia de Medici *by Angelo Bronzino*
2 Henry II as a Child *by Jean Clouet*
3 James Stuart (detail from the Children of Charles I) *by Sir Anthony Van Dyck*

PARVVLE PATRISSA, PATRIÆ VIRTVTIS ET HÆRES
ESTO, NIHIL MAIVS MAXIMVS ORBIS HABET.
GNATVM VIX POSSVNT COELVM ET NATVRA DEDISSE,
HVIVS QVEM PATRIS, VICTVS HONORET HONOS.
ÆQVATO TANTVM, TANTI TV FACTA PARENTIS,
VOTA HOMINVM, VIX QVO PROGREDIANTVR, HABENT
VINCITO, VICISTI. QVOT REGES PRISCVS ADORAT
ORBIS, NEC TE QVI VINCERE POSSIT, ERIT.   Ricard. Morysini Car.

The Knight and the Lady

The story of the young knight who arrives just in time to save the beautiful princess from being devoured by a dragon is one of the oldest tales in the world. The Greeks called the hero Perseus and endowed him with magic power. Flying with winged shoes lent him by Hermes, the messenger god, he comes down from the clouds, as shown in Piero di Cosimo's painting, and appears again, on the back of the dragon, his sword raised. Andromeda, who is seen at the left, was offered by her father because the gods had told him that only by sacrificing her could he free his country from the beast's ravages.

Centuries later the Christian St. George takes the place of the Greek Perseus. St. George's strength lies not in magic wings but in a pure heart and faith in God. Riding his white horse, he pierces the dragon with his lance before it can reach the terrified princess. The earnest young knight is dressed in full armor; his cloak blowing in the wind emphasizes the speed of his movements. The evil, liver-colored dragon writhes under his attack; the princess prays in the background; and the gay little horse looks out at you as though to assure you that everything will come out all right.

Color Plate: St. George and the Dragon *by Raphael* (Washington, National Gallery of Art)

1 St. George *by Andrea Mantegna*
2 Perseus and Andromeda (detail) *by Piero di Cosimo*

People Outdoors

It is easy to say, "paint exactly what you see," but it is hard to do. The Impressionists tried (see page 99), and developed a new way of laying on pigment to bring painted colors closer to those of nature. They found that colors appear brighter if little blobs of different colored paint are laid side by side on the canvas and looked at from a distance so that they blend in the eye of the spectator instead of being mixed on the artist's palette. They painted sparkling pictures of sunlit or foggy days, of noontime or dusk; but their world lacks solidity. Their people seem to melt into the air.

Seurat loved the bright color and weather effects of the Impressionists, but he wanted to make people solid and to arrange them in the space of his canvas. He repeated shapes over and over again, but with variety. Count the umbrellas and note their different sizes. The curve of the boat's sail resembles a tilted umbrella, as does also the line of the dog's tail. The middle woman and child, the tree trunks, and the men's tall hats are all cylinders. Instead of painting in uneven daubs, Seurat used bright little dots.

Renoir began as an Impressionist and in his paintings people dissolve in light. Seurat manages to show light and air and also a world with weight and permanence.

Color Plate: Sunday Afternoon on the Island of
La Grande Jatte *by Georges Seurat* (Chicago, Art Institute)
Small Color Plate: The Public Garden *by Pierre-Auguste Renoir*
(Oxford, Ashmolean Museum)

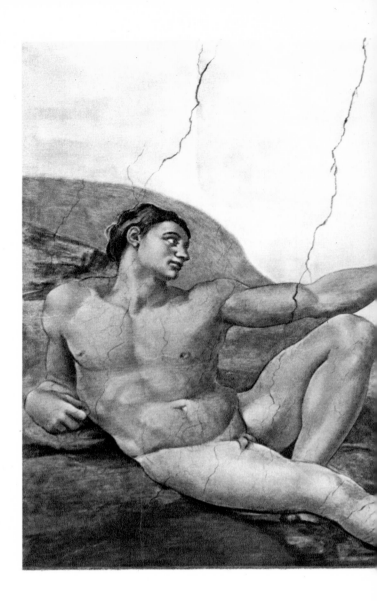

Color Plate: Creation of Man *by Michelangelo*
(Rome, Sistine Chapel)

Creation of Man

The Sistine Chapel was named for Pope Sixtus IV, who had begun the decoration of its walls with Bible scenes, but who died before the work was completed. Some twenty years later Pope Julius II commissioned Michelangelo to paint the ceiling and end wall. They were to be done in fresco, which is watercolor on the wet plaster of a wall or ceiling, a durable kind of painting but exhausting for the artist.

First Michelangelo made his plan on paper, sketching individual figures and details. Then, having erected a staging in the sixty-foot-high room, he lay on his back on the topmost boards to draw the scenes on the dry ceiling. Next he covered a small part of the drawing, the amount he believed he could paint in one day, with a layer of wet plaster. Finally with a sharp tool Michelangelo redrew the main lines in the soft plaster and proceeded to lay on the colors. By night the plaster would be dry and any unfinished part would have to be scraped off. Perhaps a head or a pair of hands would be a day's work.

Imagine the labor! Ten thousand square feet to be designed, sketched, plastered, and painted with more than three hundred and forty human figures, all overhead, and all at seven stories above the floor! It took Michelangelo four and a half years to do it. He wrote

a sonnet, half bitterly, half humorously describing the sufferings he had endured.

> I've grown a goitre by dwelling in this den...
> That drives the belly close beneath the chin:
> My beard turns up to heaven; my nape falls in,
> Fixed on my spine: my breastbone visibly
> Grows like a harp: a rich embroidery
> Bedews my face from brush-drops thick and thin...

The ceiling story begins over the altar with God creating. A giant figure, supported by angels and filled with vitality and power, He separates earth and sky and calls the sun and moon into being. Then, to the physically perfect Adam whom He has made from the dust of the earth, He gives life by a touch of His finger.

Michelangelo's genius and energy as a painter are magnificently displayed in the Sistine Chapel, but painting is only one of the fields in which he excelled. He was very famous as a sculptor; he was also an able poet; and the Church of St. Peter in Rome stands as a monument to his greatness as an architect.

71

The Cold World of Winter

An opportunity for the medieval artist to paint subjects not directly connected with religion was offered by the calendar painted in prayer books or carved on cathedral portals. Each month was headed with a picture of an activity associated with that month. January was represented by feasting, March by pruning grape vines, June by mowing hay, and so on. February was symbolized by people huddling over a fire. Carved on the portal of Amiens Cathedral is an old man who has taken off his shoes to warm his feet.

Pol de Limbourg's *February* in the calendar he painted for the Duc de Berry shows a peasant farm in winter. He left off the front wall of the house so that we could see the traditional fireside scene within. In the barnyard the sheep crowd together in the fold for warmth; chickens and birds peck at scattered grain; each beehive has its cap of snow. A woman, blowing on her hands, hurries toward the house. Beyond, a man chops firewood, while another drives a load to market in the distant town. The sense of crisp, biting cold is increased by the blue sky and the shadowless snow.

A century and a half later Pieter Bruegel planned a series of paintings of the months, only five of which were finished. His *February* repeats the medieval warming scene as an incident at the left, but the main interest is the broad snowy valley, cold and still except for the hunters with their shivering dogs, the people on the ice and the flying bird.

1

2

Color Plate: February (from the "Très Riches Heures du Duc de Berry") *by Pol de Limbourg* (Chantilly, Musée Condé)

1 February: French relief, 13th century
2 February: Hunters in the Snow *by Pieter Bruegel*

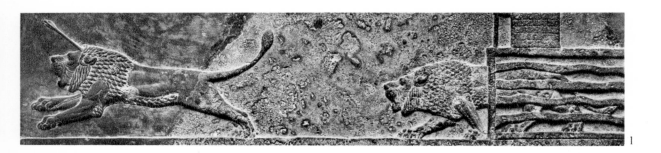

The Sport of Kings

Some people hunt for food or to destroy dangerous animals; others hunt for sport. In any case there is the thrill of matching human wits against those of an animal powerful enough to be dangerous or clever enough to cause unforeseen difficulties.

In Rubens' day hunting was considered truly the "sport of kings." Men, women, dogs and horses took part. Rubens shows the quarry—wolves and foxes—brought to bay, and the hunters closing in for the kill. The silk-clad lady and gentleman (said to be Rubens and his wife) will be protected from any real danger by the servants on foot.

The pampered king of ancient Assyria underwent even fewer of the hardships of the hunt. Trapped lions were brought in cages and released for him to shoot.

But to the American backwoodsman in Homer's painting, alone with his dogs, the deer means food and clothing and its capture proves his ability to survive in the wilds.

The English fox hunt is pure sport, offering the excitement of the chase and the opportunity to test and exhibit skill in horsemanship.

Color Plate: Wolf Hunt *by Peter Paul Rubens*
   (New York, Metropolitan Museum of Art)

1 Hunting Scene: Assyrian relief (detail),
   7th century B.C.
2 Huntsman and Dogs *by Winslow Homer*
3 Crossing the Stream *by Henry Alken*

The Many Faces of George Washington

What did Washington really look like? All the pictures on these two pages were painted by people who knew him. Each one was said by someone in Washington's day to be a good likeness—yet look at them! "But they aren't like him!" one wants to say. How do we know? There were no cameras then and we have to depend on painted portraits and descriptions to tell us what he looked like. Because it is the finest painting and shows a man of dignity and power, we think of Stuart's painting as the only true likeness—yet Stuart did not know Washington very well and he left out things that we know were there. For instance, Washington's face was scarred from smallpox and he had a mole under his ear. Both the scars and the mole are in Williams' portrait. Peale's painting was done before Washington lost his teeth and had to wear the false ones that make his mouth look so uncomfortable in Stuart's painting. Washington's personality seemed to have awed people and baffled painters. Read the description written by General Mercer in 1760 and decide for yourself which picture shows him best.

His head is well shaped, though not large, but is gracefully poised on a superb neck. A large and straight, rather than a prominent nose; blue-grey, penetrating eyes, which are widely separated and overhung by a heavy brow. His face is long rather than broad, with high rounded cheek bones, and terminates in a good firm chin. He has a clear, though a rather colorless, pale, skin... A pleasing benevolent, though a commanding countenance... His mouth is large and generally firmly closed... His features are regular and placid...

Stuart purposely never finished this painting. He kept it to copy again and again as he received orders for likenesses of Washington. It stayed in his studio until he died.

Color Plate: George Washington, 1796, *by Gilbert Stuart* (Boston, Museum of Fine Arts)

1 George Washington (detail; painted in 1789) *by Christian Gullager*
2 Washington at Princeton (detail; painted in 1784) *by Charles Willson Peale*
3 Washington as a Mason (after a painting made about 1793) *by William Williams*
4 George Washington (miniature; painted in 1793) *by John Ramage*
5 Washington at Trenton (detail; painted in 1792) *by John Trumbull*
6 George Washington (detail; painted about 1795) *by Edward Savage*

Bridges

What is the most interesting thing about a bridge? The busy life streaming across it? Its structure? Its appearance? Or all of these combined? Renoir captured the life and color of noontime bustle on a bridge that has carried busy Paris traffic since the sixteenth century.

Whistler chose to paint a London bridge at night. In his picture, the pier and the span of the bridge become great looming shadows above a boat moving soundlessly on the dark water.

What interested Stella was the way a bridge—particularly a suspension bridge—seems to leap from shore to shore, mysteriously hovering between the water that it spans and the sky above, rising strong and light and balanced.

Stella took his inspiration from Brooklyn Bridge, New York, piling up the pointed arches of its great stone piers against a background of skyscrapers. But it might be any suspension bridge at night. The flickering and slashing white lines suggest cables and car lights. The curved shapes of green and blue indicate waves and currents in the water below. Converging lines suggest passageways —for cars, for people, for trains—over the bridge, and even through subway tunnels beneath the bed of the river. The prism-like shape at the bottom of the canvas hints at the drill that penetrates the earth to bedrock for pier foundations—or perhaps, the weight on a plumb line swinging just off center. Suspension bridges have solid foundations, yet are not absolutely rigid. They sway a little in the wind.

Though there are no people in the picture, and no cars, the crisscrossing lights give us the feeling that the bridge is a center of life and movement.

1

2

Color Plate: Brooklyn Bridge *by Joseph Stella*
(New Haven, Yale University Art Gallery)

1 Battersea Bridge *by James McNeill Whistler*
(London, Tate Gallery)
2 Le Pont Neuf *by Pierre-Auguste Renoir*
(New York, Mrs. Peter Benziger Collection)

Laugh, Clown, Laugh!

In past centuries noblemen and kings used to hire jesters or "fools" as entertainers. Today circus clowns and movie or television comedians take their place. We enjoy their antics, their jokes, and their songs. But artists and poets have been haunted by the idea that a comedian cannot always feel like being funny. Under his mask of merriment what is the clown thinking?

Frans Hals probably was not much troubled by such questions. His jester is full of life and sparkle as he glances up to see whether his last joke has pleased his master. He has been accompanying himself on the lute, an instrument resembling a guitar, and his hand hovers over the strings. The broad brush strokes suggest the casual, easygoing mood of the painting. But the hand on the lute is carefully done, perhaps to suggest the sureness of the playing.

Frans Hals worked in Holland in the early seventeenth century. Watteau in France, a century later, painted the Italian comedians who traveled from one estate to another playing for families and their guests. His *Mezzetin* is gaily dressed, but his face betrays an inner sadness. The *Guitar Player* painted by Manet in the nineteenth century looks like a ragged Spanish troubadour. Does his face reflect only the mood of his song or is some tragedy hidden behind his wide eyes? Saddest of all are Picasso's clowns, who stand alone, tired and forgotten as soon as the show is over and the audience has gone home.

Color Plate: Fool with a Lute: *copy attributed to Judith Leyster after Frans Hals* (Amsterdam, Rijksmuseum)

1 Two Clowns and a Dog *by Pablo Picasso*
2 The Guitar Player *by Edouard Manet*
3 The Mezzetin *by Jean-Antoine Watteau*

"Proper Bostonians"

Color Plate: Paul Revere *by John Singleton Copley*
(Boston, Museum of Fine Arts)

1 John Hancock *by John Singleton Copley*
2 Mrs. Theodore Atkinson Jr. *by John Singleton Copley*
3 Mrs. Sylvanus Bourne *by John Singleton Copley*

Through the eyes of the painter John Singleton Copley we see the leaders of Boston in the years of the Boston Massacre, the Tea Party and the colonial congresses. Here they are: skilled craftsman, noted statesman, society belle and vigorous grandmother. Almost entirely self-taught, Copley gave solidity to his subjects by lighting one side of the face and throwing the other into heavy shadow. He worked slowly, requiring dozens of sittings of many hours each for one portrait, and excelled in painting rich brocades, elaborate laces, and polished furniture.

Paul Revere was not only an active patriot whose ride to Lexington, which "spread the alarm to every Middlesex village and farm," makes his name familiar to everyone, but also an all-round craftsman—silversmith, engraver, bell founder, and manufacturer of gunpowder. Silversmiths were highly respected and it is evidence of Copley's realism and Revere's pride in his work that Revere is shown in his shirt sleeves, his tools before him and in his hand a teapot he had made. John Hancock, whose signature on the Declaration of Independence was written large enough so that "John Bull can read my name without spectacles," the beautiful Mrs. Atkinson, whose second marriage was to follow only ten days after her first husband's death, and kindly old Mrs. Sylvanus Bourne—Copley sets them all before us just as they looked, old and young, Patriots and Tories, the people who were making our country.

"Come and Join Us"

An artist sometimes thinks of his painting as a stage on which a scene is taking place, or as showing what is going on in the other half of a room in which he and his friends are sitting. Often he tries to make us feel that we are there with him and can talk and laugh with the people he is representing. To give this effect Todeschini brought the figure of the woman close to the front of the picture; she gestures towards us and seems to follow us about with her eyes. Even her little dog cocks his ear as though he has just heard us whistle. Gerard Dou's musician has hooked back the curtain of his balcony and thrusts his violin over the ledge. His music and sword belt actually seem to project beyond the canvas.

Adriaen Brouwer, one of the Dutch "Little Masters," liked to paint the life of the tavern—people gaming, eating, or quarreling, or, as here, relaxing with their pipes over a flagon of ale. Three of the men are gesturing not at each other but at someone who like ourselves seems to be in front of them. The man in the center blows us a smoke ring. His companion to the right watches to see how we take it, and the wag behind, "laying his finger aside of his nose," winks at us. As we look we are drawn into the scene and identify ourselves with the people at whom the glances are directed.

Color Plate: Peasants Smoking
  by Adriaen Brouwer (New York, Metropolitan Museum of Art)

1 Woman and Dog *by Todeschini*
2 The Violin Player *by Gérard Dou*

Craftsmen and Mirrors

St. Eloy, a goldsmith, is looking up from his work at the fair Godebertha whose father, says the legend, had brought her to the city in search of a husband. St. Eloy, touched by her sweetness and purity, and reading her inmost desire, placed a ring on her finger with the words, "I betroth thee to Christ."

Flemish painters in the fifteenth century were interested in everything around them. They loved to linger over the brocade of a lady's dress or the starched linen of her cap. Here on the table are jeweler's scales, an inkwell, a sand shaker, coins. On the shelves are vessels made for some church, a string of beads, a branch of coral, pearls and precious stones. Rings have been slipped over rolls of parchment so they won't get lost. Because shadows would have hidden some of the details the artist has omitted many of them. He loved rich colors, the sparkle of jewels, and the glitter of gold and silver.

These artists were fascinated by the round convex mirrors of the day which reflect things in miniature. To paint them and show what they reflected took great skill. Moreover, in the mirrors we see what is happening *in front* of the picture. St. Eloy's mirror shows houses across the street and two people walking by. The mirror on the banker's table in the painting by Massys reflects a man in a window. The one behind Jan Arnolfini reflects his back and that of his wife, and two other people in the room facing them. So we see the people in the picture and also what *they* would see if they looked up.

1

Color Plate: St. Eloy as a Goldsmith *by Petrus Christus* (New York, Robert Lehman Collection)

1 A Banker and His Wife *by Quentin Massys*
2 Jan Arnolfini and His Wife (detail) *by Jan van Eyck*

2

The Tall Knight and the Fat Squire

The seventeenth-century Spanish writer Miguel Cervantes created them—Don Quixote, the nobleman with the fantastic imagination and unattainable ideals, and Sancho Panza, his hard-headed, practical squire. But it was the French artist Daumier who, two centuries later, most successfully brought them to life in paint. We see master and servant jogging along seeking knightly adventures: Don Quixote on his bony horse, tall, thin and aristocratic, and Sancho Panza, fat and earthy, trailing behind on his little donkey. Daumier does not give us exact details of their appearance. They are not individuals but types of people: the noble idealist and the peasant realist. Each one alone will get into trouble. Together they will balance each other.

To Don Quixote's gallant eye the windmills he sees flapping in the distance (outside the picture) look like giants challenging him to fight. So without further thought he readies his lance and gallops off over the fields to attack the villains. Sancho Panza, whose shouts of warning have done no good, wrings his hands in despair.

Daumier's method of painting is similar to that of Oriental art (see *Herd Boy on an Ox* below) and anticipates the cartoonist of today. He sees the important points instantly, records or exaggerates them with a few vigorous brush strokes, and indicates the less important points simply and adequately. Don Quixote's bony arm, the donkey's ear, Sancho Panza's gesture are enough to tell the story.

1

Color Plate: Sancho Panza Wringing His Hands
by Honoré Daumier (New York,
Collection of Mrs. Charles S. Payson)

1 Herd Boy on an Ox *by Mori Sosen*
2 Don Quixote and Sancho Panza
by Honoré Daumier

A Picture of Peace

Suppose someone asked you to paint *Peace*. If you are Oriental you might show someone sitting quietly and thinking, as in *Contemplation* shown at left. If you are European or American you might show people doing peaceful things.

The self-taught artist Edward Hicks, a Pennsylvania Quaker, remembered a Bible passage which runs, "The wolf shall dwell with the lamb, and the leopard shall lie down with the kid, the calf and the young lion together; and a little child shall lead them. And the cow and the bear shall feed; their young ones shall lie down together; and the lion shall eat straw like the ox..." This scene of quiet concord is what he painted. Hicks had probably never seen a lion or a leopard and even the domestic animals look quaint. Yet there is something delightful about these solemn big-eyed creatures.

But animals living in peace were not enough. Hicks wanted to show that man, too, could live happily with his fellow man. So in the background he copied (in reverse) West's famous painting of William Penn making a treaty with the Indians for the land on which Philadelphia was to be built. Through his fair and honest dealings Penn had won their enduring goodwill for his "city of brotherly love." Thus Hicks combined the peace of men with the peace of nature.

Color Plate: The Peaceable Kingdom *by Edward Hicks*
(Brooklyn Museum)

1 Contemplation *by an unknown Chinese artist, possibly Hui Tsung*
2 William Penn's Treaty with the Indians *by Benjamin West*

East Meets West

A Paris merchant in the 1850's, unpacking a shipment of china from the East, found among the wrappings some printed pictures. He showed them to an artist friend who was delighted with the unfamiliar design, the firm lines, the harmonious flat colors. Others, too, admired them and so began the enthusiasm for Japanese prints felt today.

Edgar Degas was an Impressionist (see pages 13 and 98) who painted exactly what he saw, but he also enjoyed the unusual Oriental point of view. His favorite subject, the ballet, could be fitted into the Oriental pattern. An Eastern artist would show such a scene from above, so Degas places us in a box looking down on the stage. From this height the ballerina coming forward for her curtain call appears foreshortened and, in the brilliant spotlight, flattened. She is painted, like Japanese figures, without shadows. The bit of stage looks very like the slanted view in a Japanese print. In the wings we glimpse the legs of the director and the other dancers waiting for the next act.

Other painters of the time also used Eastern ideas. In the time of Queen Victoria, Whistler dressed a sitter in one of the newly fashionable kimonos and called her *The Princess of the Porcelain Country*. Bright flat colors edged with heavy lines in the Japanese manner were used by the French painter Gauguin in his *Self-Portrait*.

Color Plate: The Dancer *by Edgar Degas*
(Paris, Louvre)

1 Self-Portrait *by Paul Gauguin*
2 The Princess of the Porcelain Country
   by James McNeill Whistler
3 Two Girls Playing Cat's Cradle: color woodcut
   by Harunobu

Heir to the Throne

Don Baltasar Carlos was the darling of Spain. The only son of King Philip IV, he was strong, intelligent, winsome, a promising heir. Velásquez, the court painter, did the first portraits of the baby prince when he was between one and two years old. He is dressed in the stiff clothes fashionable in formal Spain and holds a baton, symbol of power.

At five Baltasar Carlos was an accomplished horseman, and king and courtiers took great pride in his skill. The color plate we show here is a study for a painting and therefore has a casual quality that official portraits lack. The little prince is in the courtyard of the riding academy about to begin practice. Shadowy figures move about in the background and watch from a window. But the artist's interest is in the prince: the dignity of his pose, his rich costume, and his wistful face under the white-plumed hat.

Baltasar Carlos was six when the painting was done which shows him in hunting clothes, firmly grasping his miniature gun, a great dog drowsing at his feet.

By the time he was ten government officials were making plans for his marriage, and Velásquez and his assistants were kept busy painting portraits to be sent to kings with eligible daughters. The portrait above may be one that was sent to Ferdinand of Austria to whose daughter, Mariana, Baltasar Carlos became engaged. It was a sad day for Spain and a tragic blow to his proud father when, at sixteen, the prince died.

Color Plate: Prince Baltasar Carlos at the Riding Academy *by Velásquez* (London, Wallace Collection)

1 Prince Baltasar Carlos in Hunting Costume *by Velásquez*
2 Prince Baltasar Carlos Aged Ten *attributed to Velásquez*
3 Prince Baltasar Carlos as a Baby *by Velásquez*

Children in Silks and Satins

British artists of the eighteenth century loved to paint the children of the nobility, clean, well-dressed, with rosy cheeks and shining eyes. Philosophers were convinced that childhood was the happiest time of life, that a perfect world would result if children could be allowed to grow up naturally. "Heaven lies about us in our infancy," wrote the poet Wordsworth in 1807.

To emphasize their closeness to nature children were painted sitting on the ground, usually under a tree. Simple naturalness was the theme, but the naturalness of angelic innocence, seldom of roguish mischief. Individual likeness was unimportant. Virginia planters sometimes sent written descriptions of their children to artists in England with orders for portraits and were quite satisfied with the results. What was required was a likeness to the ideal of childhood and to an aristocratic social class, and in securing this such British painters as Raeburn and Reynolds were most successful.

Small Color Plate: The Age of Innocence *by Sir Joshua Reynolds* (London, National Gallery)
Color Plate: Boy with a Rabbit *by Sir Henry Raeburn* (London, Burlington House)

Trains and Stations

Turn yourself into an eye and paint exactly what you see, said the Impressionists. As they looked they concluded that what they saw was light reflected from objects. The real subject of their picture, they decided, must be colored light. Monet said, further, that since his subject was light, and light changed incessantly, the same object would make a different picture if done in the early morning, at noon, in mid-afternoon or at dusk. So he painted haystacks, Rouen Cathedral, the Gare St. Lazare in Paris, over and over again at different times of the day.

Railroad stations in 1877 were smoky and sooty, but Monet delighted in the steam and smoke, the light falling through the skylight contrasting with the shimmering outside air. Subjects usually considered ugly looked beautiful to the Impressionists, since the light they reflected was beautiful.

Monet had studied Turner's *Rain, Steam and Speed* and learned much from the way it was painted; but Turner had tried to catch the feeling of the train in motion, while Monet merely wanted to record its appearance in light.

In the United States artists can see engines thunder over more track than in any other country in the world. Like Turner, Kansas-born Thomas Benton tried to render speed and power. He tips the engine forward, using distortion in order to secure his effect.

Color Plate: The Railroad Station (Gare St. Lazare)
   by Claude Monet (New York,
   Maurice Wertheim Collection)

1 Power (detail) *by Thomas Hart Benton*
2 Rain, Steam and Speed *by J. M. W. Turner*

Color Plate: The Adoration of the Magi
  by Albrecht Dürer (Florence, Uffizi)

1 Iris: drawing *by Albrecht Dürer*
2 Beetle: drawing *by Albrecht Dürer*
3 A Wise Man's Gift: drawing
  by Albrecht Dürer

The Gifts of the Magi

Long before the feast of Christmas was celebrated, the coming of the three wise men was a great Church festival. Their visit to Bethlehem was important because it was the first time that the infant Jesus was shown to people outside the village in which He was born. The wise men were thought of as representing all mankind. From early times they appear in art as a young man, a middle-aged man, and an old man. Later they are named Balthazar, Melchior and Caspar. By the fifteenth century they are also of three races, black, white and yellow. Since they came from the East, supposed to be a region of great riches, they are usually robed in gorgeous silks and attended by turbaned servants, hunting dogs and pet monkeys. Eventually people came to think of them as kings, so they appear wearing jeweled crowns. Their gifts have meaning. Gold was the symbol of Christ's heavenly kingship; frankincense, used in worship, the symbol of His godhead; and myrrh, a burial spice, stood for His manhood.

These were ideas that the Church expected every artist to include in paintings of the Epiphany, but he could present them in his own way. Dürer loved detail. He painted the pavement stones, the goldwork of the gifts, the brocade of the garments, even the beetle (in the lower right-hand corner) and the butterflies on the flowers. How carefully he studied these things is proved by the sketches from his notebooks.

1

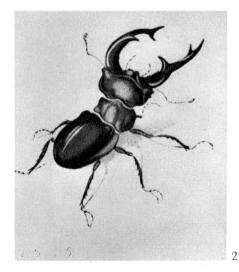

2

3

Man against Beast

To the western world the lion is the "king of beasts"—lithe and powerful but also sinister and dangerous. The calmness with which Ashurbanipal stabs his rearing victim was intended to show his greatness as man and king. Heroes like Hercules and Samson proved their prowess by killing lions. Such scenes gave artists the opportunity to depict tense excitement and also to symbolize man's superiority over beast or even the triumph of good over evil.

Delacroix had something of this in mind when he painted struggles between men and animals. His native land, France, was going through one bloody revolution after another. Delacroix wanted to show people fighting for their lives, but instead of painting Frenchmen in arms he took his subjects from distant countries, such as Greece or Morocco, or from times long past, such as the Middle Ages, and showed different kinds of battles and conflicts. In *Arab Rider Attacked by a Lion* he suggests the desperateness of the struggle between man and beast by sinuous lines and swift brush strokes, by the use of hot colors—reds and oranges—handled so that even the blues and greens, which are usually considered cool colors, look hot.

Fighting horsemen was the theme of a lost battle-painting by Leonardo da Vinci, known through a copy made by Rubens. Delacroix had studied the way it was drawn, and used similar close-packed bodies and interlacing curves.

Color Plate: Arab Rider Attacked by a Lion
   by Eugène Delacroix (Chicago, Art Institute)

1 Battle of Anghiari, *copy by Rubens after Leonardo da Vinci*

2 King Ashurbanipal Killing a Lion: Assyrian relief (detail), 7th century B.C.

The Giant-Killer

Color Plate: The Youthful David *by Andrea del Castagno* (Washington, National Gallery of Art)

1 David: statue in bronze *by Andrea Verrocchio*
2 David Fighting Goliath: manuscript, 15th century
3 David and Goliath: silver plate, 7th century

Too young to fight in the army, David came to camp with food for his brothers. There every day he saw the giant Goliath challenge anyone to fight him. David had no armor, sword, or spear, but he had the sling with which he had managed to kill a lion and a bear that attacked his father's sheep. So, taking five smooth stones from the brook, he went out to meet Goliath. The giant laughed and taunted him, but before he could throw his spear David slung a stone at Goliath's forehead, knocked him down, and with the giant's own sword cut off his head.

David was a symbol of the national hero who wins victory for his people against great odds. He appears sometimes as a child, sometimes as a full grown man, now in Roman dress, now as a medieval prince. The Italians of the Renaissance found in his athletic young figure opportunity to study the body in action or at rest. Castagno was a leader in this scientific investigation. He has chosen a difficult pose—David striding to the left, but turning, his hand outthrust, to the right. Drawing the left foot and outstretched arm in such positions was a new and difficult problem. The curious shape of Castagno's painting results from its having been done on a tournament shield.

Verrocchio's youth stands meditative over the head of his victim, his softly molded face and wiry arms those of a teenage boy.

2

3

The Frolicking God
and his Princess

1

2

Color Plate: Bacchus and
Ariadne *by Titian*
(London, National Gallery)

1 Dionysus Sailing over the Sea:
detail from vase by Exekias,
6th century B.C.
2 Marriage of Bacchus and
Ariadne *by Tintoretto*

Bacchus, the god of wine, called Dionysus by the
Greeks, was also a lawgiver and peacemaker. On
an ancient Greek dish we see him in a ship under a
grape-laden vine traveling over the sea to bring the
arts of civilization to mankind.

Titian's painting tells the story of his meeting
with Ariadne, a legendary princess. Bacchus frol-
icked one day in the woods with fat, jolly Silenus,
his friend and teacher, with nymphs who played
cymbals and tambourines and with satyrs who were
half man, half goat. As Bacchus came out of the
forest he saw Ariadne, who, frightened, turned to
run away. Bacchus was so taken by her beauty that
he pursued and won her.

Titian has arranged this picture of the meeting
of god and princess with the greatest care. The
exact center is marked by the white flower at the
bottom straddled by the sturdy baby satyr. The
dark, crowded half of the picture contrasts with the
light, empty half. Yet the halves balance each other
because the emptier one contains Ariadne and
Bacchus' head and shoulders. These two, the artist
seems to say, equal in importance all the followers
of Bacchus put together. The young god with his
flying cape links the two halves. Over Ariadne's
head is the star-crown which Bacchus gave her as
a wedding present.

Tintoretto constructed his painting of the marriage of Bacchus and Ariadne as carefully as Titian
did the scene of their meeting. The lovers, together
with Venus, goddess of Love, are arranged in a sort
of wheel of which the wedding ring held by Bacchus
is the hub. Their arms form the spokes, while
Ariadne's back, the floating figure of Venus, and
Bacchus' left arm make the rim.

Mother and Child

1

Artists have always loved to paint mothers with their babies, but when that mother is Mary and the baby is Jesus there are many problems to solve. Shall the artist make Mary like his own wife, holding their baby son in her arms? That is what Gari Melchers has done. Or shall he make her greater than human mothers, adored by saints, holding a child who is calm and wise even in his infancy? That is what Raphael did in the painting for the monks of St. Sixtus, which has ever since been called the *Sistine Madonna*. Or shall he give her a crown and dress her in gold robes, showing her as the Queen of Heaven who crushes the devil under her feet while she plays with her smiling baby? That is the way an unknown sculptor rendered her in the sixteenth century.

Botticelli chose another kind of Mary, the Mary who "kept all these things"—the strange and wonderful things that had happened to Jesus—"and pondered them in her heart." She is beautiful and young, her golden hair showing through the thin veil over her head; but she is thoughtful, almost sad. As she touches the wheat and grapes a strangely smiling angel brings to her, she dimly foresees what suffering the future is going to bring to her child. Even the baby looks thoughtful as He raises His hand to bless the heavenly food.

2

3

Color Plate: Madonna and Child
by Botticelli (Boston, Isabella
Stewart Gardner Museum)

1 Madonna and Child:
Spanish sculpture, 16th century
2 Mother and Child
by Gari Melchers
3 Sistine Madonna *by Raphael*

Dancing in Paint

Rhythm is in the beating of our hearts, the swing of arms and legs as we walk. We feel it throughout our bodies. Its beat is essential for music and dancing. In painting it becomes visible in repetitions of lines, shapes, and colors.

Piet Mondrian wanted to paint a dance—not people dancing, but the dancing itself. As he walked along Broadway in New York, the noise and movement, the flashing lights, seemed to him to form a pattern of sound and rhythm. He found an order in the confusion of streetlights, stop-and-go signals, signs and advertisements. Each sign had its own sequence of repetitions, its own syncopations. All together produced a gigantic visual jazz: color, light, and beat joining in an exciting pattern. Behind and beneath it was the framework of streets in rectangular plan, buildings with rectangular fronts, windows and doors, and basic colors: yellow, red, and blue. Mondrian called the painting "Boogie-Woogie," for the kind of jazz that combines unexpected musical phrases with a powerful, regular rhythm. Look at the painting steadily for a few moments and you will find that the squares and rectangles literally dance before your eyes.

Renoir, on the other hand, was interested in the dancers rather than the dance. He painted them as he saw them, a man and a woman dancing together, absorbed in each other. The swirling skirt and the postures suggest the whole movement and feeling of dancing at a fair.

To Seurat in his painting of a French vaudeville dance called *Le Chahut*, the important thing was the gaiety. He captured it in the upcurved lines, in the pointing toes and in the dabs and dots of color. Three lights, four toes, two arms, and four legs, create a three-four, two-four rhythm, but the firm back of the cellist in the foreground keeps it from getting too lively.

Color Plate: Broadway Boogie-Woogie
   by Piet Mondrian (New York,
   Museum of Modern Art)

1 Dance at Bougival *by Pierre-Auguste
   Renoir* (Boston, Museum of Fine Arts)
2 Le Chahut *by Georges Seurat* (Buffalo,
   Albright Art Gallery)

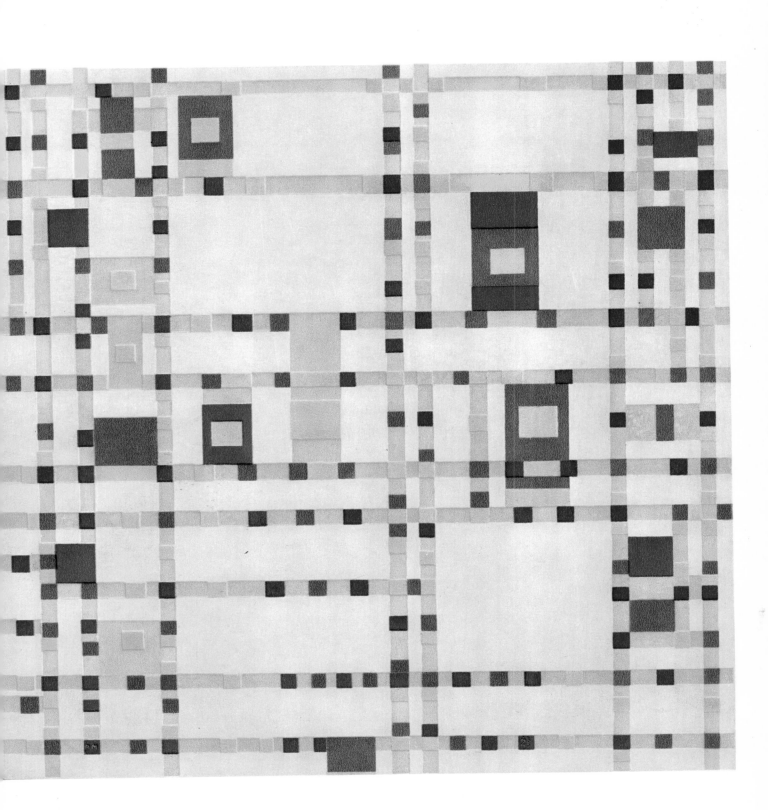

... And now you have finished the Book

And now you have finished the book. At least you have looked at the last picture and turned the last page. But a book of this kind is never finished. It can be set on your desk, open to a favorite picture—a different one each week. It is much more than just a book, it is a door to the world of art. The works reproduced here actually exist in paint or ink or stone or wood or bronze or clay. Most of them are in museums that are open to you to visit. The index will tell you where every original work is. You may go to a particular museum because you know a favorite picture is there, or you may come upon it unexpectedly and your heart will warm with the feeling that you are meeting an old friend.

Just as one friend introduces you to another, so each of these pictures can lead you to understand and enjoy others by the same artist, or of the same kind. Gradually your circle of picture-friends will grow. Perhaps you will become curious about the artists and will want to read books about their lives. Or perhaps you will want to try painting yourself and will learn the satisfaction that comes from doing creative work.

For the work of art is the product of that highest capacity of man: the capacity to think and to dream. From all that is around him the artist creates the painting which contains his thoughts and dreams. Through that painting he passes his thoughts and dreams down through the centuries and over the barriers of different languages and customs, to the mind and soul of the person of today who has learned to look and to understand.

Index of Pictures, Artists and Owners

113

Acknowledgments

The author and publishers wish to thank all individuals and institutions who cooperated in making works of art in their possession available for reproduction in this book.

Thanks is also due to the following for photographs or prints reproduced on the pages mentioned:

Messrs. Alinari, Florence, for *Infant Hercules Strangling Serpents* 25, *Hercules and the Hydra* 25, *Girls Playing Jackstones* 29, *Scrovegno Presents the Arena Chapel* 38, *The Gleaners* 38, *St. Ursula's Dream* 40, *The Fisher Girl* 52, *Wrestlers* 55, *Hercules and Antaeus* 55, *Self-Portrait* by J. B. S. Chardin 62, *The Violin Player* 84, *A Banker and His Wife* 86, *The Adoration of the Magi* 100, *David* 104; Messrs. Anderson, Rome, for *Wedding Dance* 15, *St. George and the Dragon* 21, *St. Francis Preaching to the Birds* 36, *Head of Spinola* 52, *Self-Portrait* by Elisabeth Vigée-Lebrun 62, *James Stuart* 64, *St. George* 66, *Perseus and Andromeda* 66, *Bacchus and Ariadne* 106, *Sistine Madonna* 108; Oliver Baker, New York, for *Don Manuel Osorio* 17, *The Gulf Stream* 32, *Stag at Sharkey's* 54, *St. Eloy as a Goldsmith* 87, *Sancho Panza Wringing His Hands* 89, *The Peaceable Kingdom* 91, *The Railroad Station* 98; Dr. Buchtal and the Warburg Institute, London, for *David Playing the Harp* 19; Franz Hanfstaengl, Munich, for *Red Horses* 23 (copyright 1926), *The Fifer* 44, *Fool with a Lute* 80; Foto Kleinhempel, Hamburg, for *Revolution of the Viaduct* 27; Arthur Jaffé, Inc., for *Sunday Afternoon on the Island of La Grand Jatte* 69; Peter A. Juley & Son, New York, for *The Spielers* 29, *Power* 99; Frank Lerner, New York, for *The Card Players* 35; Messrs. W. F. Mansell, London, for *Officers of St. George's Company* 30, *Piper and Drummer* 45; Mrs. Arthur Morrison for *Horses* 23, *Herd Boy on an Ox* 88; The Phillips Studio, Philadelphia, for *William Penn's Treaty with the Indians* 90; Soichi Sunami for *Lady Jean* 8, *Katharine Cornell* 60; Studio Publications for *Harmony* from *Nura's Children Go Visiting* 19; J. K. Tannheuser for *Two Clowns and a Dog* 81; Twin Editions, New York, for *St. Francis in Ecstasy* 37; Charles Uht, New York, for *Le Pont Neuf* 78; Sir Robert Witt for *Boy with a Kite* 29, *Dutch Interior* 46, *The Battle of Anghiari* 102.

The author is especially grateful to Miss Roberta Yerkes, whose criticism of text and ready assistance in matters of form have been of incalculable value.

DESIGNED BY ULRICH RUCHTI